Social and Antisocial Development

by
Martin Herbert

BPS Blackwell

© Martin Herbert 2002
A BPS Blackwell book

Editorial Offices:
108 Cowley Road, Oxford OX4 1JF, UK
  Tel: +44 (0)1865 791100
350 Main Street, Malden, MA 02148-5018, USA
  Tel: +1 781 388 8250

First published 2002 by The British Psychological Society and Blackwell Publishers Ltd, a Blackwell Publishing company

Library of Congress Cataloging-in-Publication Data has been applied for

ISBN 1 85433 358 5 (paperback)

A catalogue record for this title is available from the British Library.

Set in Lapidary
by Ralph J. Footring, Derby
Printed and bound in Great Britain
by T J International, Padstow, Cornwall

For further information on
Blackwell Publishers, visit our website:
www.blackwellpublishers.co.uk

Contents

Social and antisocial development

Children are travellers newly arrived in a
strange country of which they know nothing.
John Locke

Introduction

My purpose in this guide is:

➤ to describe some of the features of vulnerable children and adolescents,
  their early circumstances, and developmental pathways on the way to
  antisocial behaviour;
➤ to discuss the development of pro-social behaviour in the adolescent – a
  period of development that tends to be 'demonized' in the media and,
  indeed, in the minds of many parents;
➤ to provide an empirical account of the nature of adolescence as a modest
  counter to the gloom and nihilism of the apocalyptic view of the younger
  generation;
➤ to explore the meaning of effective parenting;
➤ to describe the ways in which professionals can assess problem behaviour
  and, if appropriate, intervene.

To these ends, I will review a range of behavioural methods and their success
in producing effective child management in families with children who are
exhibiting moderate to high levels of disruptive, antisocial and aggressive
behaviour.

Aims

This book will provide the practitioner with:

➤ a brief account of the development of social and antisocial development
  in childhood and adolescence;
➤ a review of effective interventions available to professionals and parents.

Objectives

After reading this guide the practitioner should be familiar with:

➤ some of the main features of social development in childhood and adolescence;
➤ some of the factors in the development of antisocial behaviour;
➤ some common interventions for problem behaviour(s) and their effectiveness.

Part I: Adolescence – leaving childhood behind

Somewhere between the immaturity of childhood and the hoped-for maturity of adulthood lie the six or more years referred to as adolescence. If there is any one event that makes adolescence stand out from the rest of childhood, it is the radical nature of the growth that occurs at that time. These physical, physiological and mental changes transform children into adults. Many of the significant psychological changes (e.g. mature self-awareness) appear to be related to the teenager's physical and cognitive maturing. Adolescence begins, it is said, in biology (at puberty) and ends in culture (when young people take on an independent existence). It is, for these reasons, a moveable feast and one stretching over several years. Given that it is such a lengthy stage of life, it is best divided into early, middle and late adolescence. I will concentrate mainly on early and middle adolescence, in other words, children from about 11 to 16.

That there is (and is bound to be in contemporary society) a stage of transition from emotional and social 'irresponsibility' to mature and responsible citizen has been widely, but not universally, accepted. Some cultures, notably preliterate ones, have 'rites of passage' that take children directly from their childhood to adult status. There are theorists who reject the notion of adolescence as a distinct stage of development; they repudiate the idea that, at puberty, every child somehow takes on a qualitatively different persona or engages in radically different developmental tasks, more or less overnight. Rather, they argue, the child grows by imperceptible degrees into a teenager, and the adolescent turns by degrees into an adult. Others disagree. The confusion over the boundaries defining adolescence is revealed by the metaphors applied to it: the 'in-between stage' and 'that no-man's land between childhood and adolescence'. It has also been referred to as a tunnel into which young people disappear. They are then 'lost to sight' for a few years. According to this metaphor you never know what is going to emerge at the other end – a daunting prospect for parents and teachers (if true) when they have put so much time, effort and affection, into preparing the children in their care for adulthood and citizenship. What then are the facts?

Sheep in wolf's clothing?

Many parents await their child's approaching adulthood with a sense of foreboding. They anticipate the adolescent years as something to be endured rather than enjoyed, to be confronted rather than shared. It is often the case that they are apprehensive that they may 'lose' the closeness, the affection and the degree of parental control they feel to be important in their relationship with their son or daughter.

Hutter (1938) described adolescence in *Alice in Wonderland* terms as a period of development 'in which normally abnormalities so often happen it is abnormal that everything passes normally'. Anna Freud (1958, p. 8) said it was 'abnormal' if a child kept a 'steady equilibrium during the adolescent period.... The adolescent manifestations come close to symptom formation of the neurotic, psychotic or dissocial order and merge almost imperceptibly into ... almost all the mental illnesses'. As a final illustration of the medical view of adolescence as pathology, we have van Krevelen (1971), who wrote that 'adolescence is a period of life, which by its disintegrative character may seem a psychosis in itself ... it is difficult to discern in this stage a pathological process from normal development'.

The empirical evidence is more prosaic. The findings, based on small-scale investigations and large-scale surveys of 'run-of-the-mill' adolescents (rather than the biased impressions of clinicians, who mainly see disturbed or deviant young people), is that adolescence can usually be negotiated by children with intuitive, sensible parents and reasonably benign socio-economic backgrounds with relatively little fuss (e.g. Coleman and Hendry, 1999; Nielsen, 1987; Rutter, 1979). If approached in the right frame of mind, adolescence can be a period of relatively harmonious relationships – or at least as harmonious as most other stages of development. This requires an acceptance of the essential continuity of important aspects of the personality from childhood, through adolescence, and on to adulthood: the 'changeling' phenomenon – in the sense of some radical change – is somewhat unusual.

The 'storm and stress' view of adolescence

The teenage phase, while certainly not immune from its share of pain for those growing up (and for those guiding the growing-up processes), is not usually characterized by severe emotional disturbance. Nevertheless, transition and change are features of adolescence. An understanding of these processes can be of benefit, especially if they 'normalize' parental attributions (attitudes and theories) by repudiating some of the popular myths.

Psychological problems are probably a little commoner during adolescence than during middle childhood, but the difference is not very great; some 10–15 per cent of adolescents experience significant psychological problems. These figures are close to rates at other stages of development (Graham and Rutter, 1973). What makes for a lot of difference is that 'deviant' behaviour or risky activities at this stage of life carry greater potential 'penalties', some long lasting, irreversible, even life threatening. Experiments with drugs, sex, truancy or delinquent activities can carry heavy costs, as parents know only too well.

At a more mundane level of parental worries, the generation gap is one of the popular conceptions that does not live up to expectations. Labels are misleading because they suggest distinctions that are absolute rather than matters of degree. If anything, it could be said that the generations are drawing together rather than apart. Adolescents and their parents tend to agree on the important issues more than do parents and their parents (grandparents).

People have been led to believe that the 'distancing' (alienation) of young adults from their parents means that they may not be able to communicate with their children when they get older. Distancing is not, however, a typical pattern. Most adolescents are still attached to their homes in a positive way, and they continue to depend upon the emotional support, goodwill and approval of their parents. The family continues to be of critical importance to them, as it was in earlier, less mature years; indeed, concern and supervision (as long as it is not oppressive or too intrusive) can be demonstrated to be vital during a phase when youngsters are experimenting with identities, indeed with life. Emotional (i.e. personal) support is important as the young person deals with changes in body image (during the 'growth spurt'), changes in hormonal activity and the increasing challenge of more complex developmental (e.g. academic and social) tasks.

It is exceptional for teenagers to feel torn between their two 'worlds' of parents and peers, certainly on the more important issues of life such as politics or education. There are most likely to be differences of opinion on minor issues such as hairstyle, fashion, social habits and privileges, where parental views are likely to be rejected in favour of the standards of the peer group. Parents tend, often, to suffer from 'selective amnesia', a condition that allows them to forget their own adolescent fads and fashions, and the distaste they aroused in their mothers and fathers.

Cognitive development

By the end of middle childhood, we begin to see the fundamental difference between the rather restricted and immature thinking of early childhood and the cognitive capabilities of the stage called 'formal propositional thinking'. The difference is essentially to do with the real and the possible. It is during adolescence, roughly the years from 11 or 12 to 15, that children begin to free their thinking from its roots in their own particular experience. They become capable of general propositional thinking; that is to say, they can propose hypotheses and deduce consequences. Their language is now fast and versatile. Not unnaturally, they wish to flex their new intellectual 'muscles' and try them out in arguments with parents and teachers. Mark Twain captures the patronizing attitudes teenagers can show to the intellectual 'limitations' of their parents in their newfound abilities. Their idealism may cause them to make unflattering comments about their parents' world-weary opinions.

> When I was fourteen my father was so stupid I could hardly stand to have him around. At twenty-one I was astonished at how much he had learned in the past seven years.

There are some interesting differences in the nature of intellectual functioning in boys and girls, although it is difficult to separate out heredity and environment as causes of these differences. Intellectually, girls get off to a good start – being slightly ahead of boys on intelligence tests during the first four years of life. They literally have the first word (on average) and, one might note, because of the longevity of females, the last one too! They are more articulate. They learn to read more easily. Girls are also on a quicker physical developmental timetable than boys. The intellectual differential soon vanishes at school, although girls still excel on verbal fluency tests – using more words, telling longer stories and in fact giving support to the stereotype that females talk more than males. It is not until high school that boys draw ahead of girls on mathematical skills. Boys do better than girls on tests of spatial ability and to some extent on abstract, analytical types of reasoning.

The body and self-image

> Lousy stinking school on Thursday. I tried my old uniform on, but I have outgrown it so badly that my father is being forced to buy me a new one tomorrow. He is going up the wall but I can't help it if my body is in a growth period can I? I am only five centimetres shorter than Pandora now. My thing remains static at twelve centimetres.
> Sue Townsend: *The Secret Diary of Adrian Mole, Aged 13¾*

Young Adrian Mole, long-suffering 'offspring' of author Sue Townsend's imagination, displays in this excerpt from his diary a concern with three interrelated preoccupations that are characteristic of adolescence: his developing body and self-image, and the much repeated 'I' of self-absorption. The fragment encapsulates six of the important sources of influence on the young person's search for identity: bodily changes, genitalia, school, relationships with parents and, not least, himself and the opposite sex.

If there is any one event that makes adolescence stand out from the rest of childhood, it is the radical nature of the growth that occurs at that time. These physical, physiological and mental changes transform children into adults. Many of the significant psychological changes appear to be related to the teenager's physical and cognitive maturing. For both sexes there is an increase in size of shoulders and hips, arms and legs, height and total body weight. Boys undergo a significant increase in their muscle tissue and strength, whereas girls develop more fatty tissue, producing their softer and more rounded contours.

Puberty may bring about a degree of self-centredness in the child. The very ground on which the young person has been standing so securely until now begins to shift. The body the child has taken for granted becomes the focus of attention; so much is happening! Not surprisingly, there is a lot of mirror-gazing and minute scrutiny of blemishes and 'good points'. The physical changes of puberty, which continue for about two years, have a significant impact on the erstwhile child's body image and, building on that foundation, self-image. Parents sometimes become over-concerned when their children become egocentric and self-absorbed.

The many physical upheavals encountered during puberty require children to focus in on themselves while they adapt to change and come to terms with their new (or modified) body image (a matter we return to). It is like the canoeist who paddles along in serene waters, able to attend to all manner of things and people around, and then is suddenly swirling about in the white waters of the rapids – all concentration and energies are needed to keep the canoe upright and to maintain some reasonably safe direction. Some degree of self-absorption at such a time would seem eminently adaptive and reasonable. Of course, self-absorption can be taken to an extreme, as we shall see.

Young people also absorb the attitudes of others towards their body and its parts. They may develop a body concept that is pleasing and satisfying, or they may come to view their body and its parts as off-putting, dirty or shameful – a matter for self-deprecation. Poor self-esteem is a thread running through a large number of child and adolescent problems, ranging from drug addiction and suicidal feelings to depression and delinquent behaviour. Youngsters' favourable or unfavourable views of themselves – their self-image – and perception of, and relationship with, other people are important indications of the sort of adaptation they are making to life.

Each of us has an image of our actual (or real) self and an idealized self – ourselves as we would like to be. When there is a large discrepancy between the teenager's self-concept ('myself as I am') and his or her idealized self ('myself as I would like to be') there is also likely to be anxiety and over-sensitiveness, in close attendance. That the self-concept plays a central role can be seen in the index of most books on developmental psychology. A typical list of its many facets is as follows:

➢ self-awareness;
➢ self-control;
➢ self-disclosure;
➢ self-efficacy
➢ self-esteem;
➢ self-fulfilling prophecies;
➢ self-perception.

Identity formation

A popular belief about adolescence is that a crisis over personal identity occurs at this time, producing all or some of the symptoms of stress: anxiety, depression, a sense of frustration, conflict and defeatism. The development of identity does not always proceed smoothly, but what evidence we have calls into question the widespread belief that adolescents *usually* suffer a crisis over their identity. Most teenagers actually have a positive, but not unrealistically inflated, self-image and this view of themselves tends to be fairly stable over the years (Coleman *et al.*, 1977).

Erik Erikson proposes four ways in which adolescents arrive at a sense of who and what they are, and the problems that may ensue when the timetable is awry.

➢ *Foreclosure*. Parents or authority figures in the community inculcate ideas (vocational, political, ethnocentric and religious) which the adolescent submissively accepts. The values endorsed tend to be authoritarian, but are often delinquent when the peer group (gang) holds sway.
➢ *Identity diffusion*. The young person, devoted to fun and excitement and 'living for the day', makes no firm commitment to personal, social, political and vocational plans or beliefs.
➢ *Moratorium*. A number of roles are 'tried out' before arriving at a settled identity. Along the way (sometimes a period of considerable duration)

delinquent or unconventional (opting out) identities may be assumed before a stable sense of self is arrived at.

➤ *Achieving a clear sense of identity.* This entails the achievement (not premature or too long delayed) of a strong commitment to a consistent value system and a 'healthy' adjustment to the world of significant relationships, work and leisure.

Erikson (1965) sets out the stages of identity development as shown in Figure 1.

An assessment based, *inter alia*, on this model allows the practitioner to evaluate the teenager's adaptation to changes in his/her development, in terms of a 'timetable' of mature versus immature identity formation. This, as Figure 1 illustrates, provides an indication of vulnerability to neurotic or delinquent influences (i.e. 'unhealthy' developments).

Hormonal changes

Puberty, of course, is not just a matter of changes in the size and shape of the body. Physiological developments in glandular secretion, particularly those affecting sexual function, occur. Males and females have similar quantities of both sex hormones in the bloodstream before puberty, with only a slightly greater proportion of the sex-relevant hormone. Thus boys have nearly as much oestrogen (the female sex hormone) as androgen (the male sex hormones). At puberty, however, there is a sharp increase in the secretion of the sex-related hormone. The pituitary gland at the base of the brain starts to produce two hormones, the gonadotrophic hormones, which it releases into the bloodstream. These complex chemical substances are actually the same in both sexes; in boys they are produced together continuously, whereas in girls they are produced one after the other in accordance with the monthly menstrual cycle.

At puberty girls are, on average, two years ahead of boys in development. In typical boys there is roughly a five-year variation in the age at which puberty is reached. One of the main indicators is ejaculation or emission. By the age of 16, the average boy is fully developed sexually and is capable of becoming a father. The word 'testis' comes from the Latin for 'witness'. The presence of testicles was a witness to a man's virility and his potential as a father.

Adolescent sexuality

Hormonal changes bring in their wake behavioural changes: teenagers will have to manage the dramatic heightening of sexual awareness and increased sexual arousal; parents will have to deal with their offspring's increased (and,

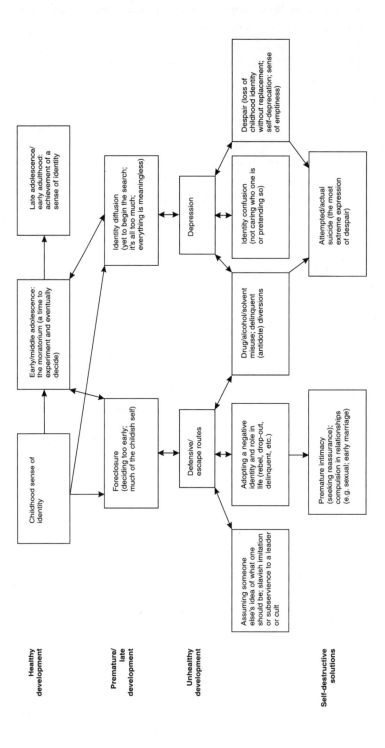

Figure 1. Stages of identity development (based upon Erikson, 1965).

in part, hormone-driven) assertiveness. The *National Survey of Sexuality and Lifestyles* presents several important findings about how adolescents in the UK express their sexuality (see Carr, 2001). The secretion of testosterone, in some males, *drives* them beyond assertion to displays of aggression, often associated with sexual activity.

Sexual behaviour may occur earlier nowadays but not that much has changed. Parents are not necessarily being old-fashioned, hypocritical or puritanical if they disapprove of, or have reservations about, teenagers having a 'sex life'. Many are afraid that youngsters might be hurt or exploited if they embark on a sexual relationship too soon, before they are more experienced and emotionally mature. What puts particular pressure on parents is their perception of some of the awful risks their children may confront at this age: unwanted pregnancies, the exploitation of naiveté and innocent emotions, and exually transmitted disease, not least AIDS (see Carr, 2001).

The incidence of teenage pregnancies (which often tend to have un-favourable social and emotional consequences) is higher in the USA than in Canada and most European nations. The UK has the highest teenage preg-nancy rate in Europe, and one of the highest of any industrialized country. A significant proportion of young women conceive more than once in their teens; one in eight who have their first baby in their teens go on to have a second child before they reach the age of 20. One in six teenagers who had an abortion in 1997 had previously had an abortion or a live birth. Eight thous-and of the 90,000 adolescents who become pregnant in the UK every year are under 16; 2200 are 14 or younger. Three-fifths of conceptions, about 56,000, result in live births.

Between a third and a half of sexually active adolescents do not use contraceptives during first sexual intercourse. One in five sexually active American teenagers contracts a sexually transmitted disease (STD) such as syphilis, gonorrhoea, chlamydia, genital herpes or AIDS. There is evidence of an association between very early sexual activity and social disadvantage, as well as antisocial behaviour.

Conclusion

It is helpful to remember that children do not face the 'hurdles' of adolescent development all at one time. Different challenges (e.g. sexuality, new relation-ships, changes in body and self-image, identity and independence issues) are spread out over several years. Children have strengths; they generally bring forward into maturity their positive attributes. They do not suddenly lose those characteristics which most parents have so assiduously nurtured. They also develop new intellectual, social and emotional capacities. They are capable of more flexible, abstract problem solving.

The enigma of adolescence for professionals and parents alike is the inability, or refusal, of teenagers to articulate and share their concerns and worries. The many positive aspects of this phase of life are often overlooked, submerged by prejudices about the 'terrible teens'. While it is true that the problems of a minority can be really daunting, and may require expert help, the majority of youngsters, if treated empathically, are there to be enjoyed by parents rather than endured.

Part II: Antisocial behaviour

> The children who need love the most will always ask for it in the most unloving way.
> (Retired teacher to mother of a hyperactive child, quoted by Barkley, 1995)

There is a mounting tide of public concern about antisocial and disruptive behaviour in young people. Of particular concern to the community is the feeling that much of it has a mindless quality that seems to defy comprehension. Reports in the media of parents being unable to control their children, of aggressive behaviour at school (bullying and blackmail of peers, attacks on teachers) and the flouting of norms and laws in the form of vandalism, muggings and hooliganism on the streets sound a note of hysteria and moral panic.

Pessimists paint a sombre picture of growing numbers of poorly socialized young people who have scarcely acquired the rudiments of human culture. They opine that the most alarming aspect is the sharp increase in crime, violence and wanton destruction of all kinds, with larger proportionate increases as one goes down the age scale. The 1996 statistics for offenders convicted or cautioned for an indictable offence indicate that 10–15-year-olds accounted for some 14 per cent of known offenders, and 10–17-year-olds were for around 25 per cent. This does represent an increase in the incidence of criminality among youth. A small hard core of persistent offenders is responsible for a disproportionate amount of crime.

It is significant that between one-half and two-thirds of all children and adolescents referred to mental health services are assessed as having disruptive behaviour disorders. These include the so-called oppositional defiant and conduct disorders. Thirty per cent of general practice consultations involving children are for behaviour problems; 45 per cent of community child health referrals are concerned with poisonings and self-harm, which are particularly frequent in children who manifest antisocial behaviour and conduct disorder.

A profile of children with antisocial disorders

So, what is meant by antisocial behaviour? Aren't all children naughty, defiant or oppositional some of the time? Of course, there is a sense in which all very young children are asocial or antisocial. What happens, as children mature, is that they have to learn to avoid certain behaviours and adopt others; that is to say, they must be trained to check certain impulses and to regulate their behaviour in terms of certain informal and formal rules of conduct. Most children are disobedient at times, or go through disobedient phases; but some take to an extreme their antagonism to parental requests and commands. Toddlers are notorious for opposing the will of their parents, and in extreme cases may be assessed as displaying oppositional defiant disorder. So intense is the resistance that at times it becomes quite clear that the child is not merely failing to comply, but is displaying a pattern of negativistic behaviour (a form of aggressive defiance) that is antipathetic to that child's ongoing social and moral development.

The clinical terms oppositional defiant disorder (ODD) and conduct disorder (CD) refer to a heterogeneous category of antisocial disruptive behaviour disorders with the common theme of an *extreme* failure of the individual to conform to the expectations of caregivers (parents), teachers or to societal norms. The behaviours can range from endless conflicts with authority (e.g. non-compliance, defiance and argumentativeness) and violations of social norms (e.g. truancy, running away from home) to serious violations of the rights of others (e.g. aggression, vandalism, fire setting, stealing and even murder).

How is the child with ODD or CD to be distinguished from the troublesome, naughty or difficult child? The answer lies in the extremeness of the behaviour: its pervasiveness, frequency, intensity and the number of co-existing deviant activities (Herbert, 1987).

Case illustration

Scott had displayed aggressive, defiant behaviour of an extreme nature since he was a toddler. Although initially they were told by professionals he would 'outgrow' these problems, his parents found he became increasingly aggressive and defiant. He was expelled from four nursery groups before he started school. The parents reported that they had tried every discipline strategy they could think of, such as time-out, yelling, hitting and taking away privileges, and grounding him. The parents reported feeling isolated and stigmatized by other parents with more 'normal' children and felt that his teachers blamed them for his misbehaviours.

An evaluation of his behaviour at school revealed inattentiveness and distractibility in the classroom, aggression towards his peers – particularly during breaks – and frequent reports of teacher calls to his mother to take him home from school because of unacceptable and uncontrollable behaviour. His intellectual performance was within the normal range yet academically he was grossly underachieving. His school absences and physical fights had resulted in frequent contact with his parents and threats of expulsion.

Society's concern about children who indulge in these kinds of activities is justified, given the pain and suffering of their victims, and not least the harm done to themselves – the perpetrators of such misery. Their antisocial behaviour is, in the end, self-destructive. It also involves great financial burdens on the community: the cost of incarceration of juvenile offenders and the costs associated with vandalism of public property. Repeated episodes of verbal and physical aggression towards other children lead to their rejection and ridicule by others – adults and children. This is a key element in the tension between parents of children with conduct disorders and parents of non-challenging children, contributing to their feelings of humiliation, rejection and isolation.

Impact on parents and others

As children approach adolescence and grow stronger, more assertive and rebellious, what were 'merely' difficult situations for parents can become menacing, and in some cases, dangerous – especially where they have been granted too much control over decisions when young. Such a burden for young people – the assumption of control when immature – is thought to cause a mixture of anxiety and extreme frustration.

Adolescents are likely to complain and compare their lot with other teenagers when the limits are set down and insisted on. However, there is clear evidence to show that children realize their parents are firm because they care. They know, deep down, that they cannot cope alone. They need to know someone has charge of their lives so that they can learn about and experiment with life from a safe base. Children who get their own way all the time tend to interpret such laissez-faire permissiveness as indifference; they feel nothing they do is important enough for their parents to bother about.

Children's invariable refusal to comply with parental requests compounds the misery. They seem to control not only the parents but also the entire family by virtue of the power they command through their wilful resistance. Many of the parents describe their children and teenagers as overactive, easily 'wound up', excitable, loud, wild and out of control – characteristics that tended to show up early on in life. Moreover, their children have trouble listening and concentrating even for brief periods. The children's activity level can be so frenetic at times as to make their safety and their survival a major parenting issue. Parents express concern about their child's inability to learn from experience. They observe their child suffering the negative conse-quences of a particular action, yet repeating the same self-defeating behaviours within a short time.

Whatever the origins of the conduct disorders (and they are many sided), the child's difficulties create a 'ripple effect' on the family, in ever-widening circles (see Webster-Stratton and Herbert, 1994). They affect first the parents, then the marital relationship, then other siblings, next the extended family and, finally, the family's relationships with the community.

Children with these problems (and their families) use multiple health, social and educational services. They are at particular risk of physical abuse. Social services departments devote most of their energies to child protection work, much of which arises from the harsh punishments meted out to children who are exceptionally difficult to manage. Residential care for children with disruptive behaviour disorders is extremely expensive and, sadly, not always caring or curative. The same can be said about the cost of the various forms of provision in the schools that are required to cope with classroom disruption.

Unfortunately, the prevalence of disruptive behavioural disorders has generated a need for services that far exceeds available resources and personnel. The consequences of such a mismatch are serious enough in the short term; one thinks of the distress that goes unalleviated for so many young people. But there is another concern: the possibility of blighted futures over the longer term. These 'aggressive', antisocial children are at increased risk of developing a veritable litany of problems later in life, such as truancy, alcoholism, drug abuse, juvenile delinquency, adult crime and interpersonal problems (see Robins and Price, 1991). Paradoxically, in the UK, children with less serious difficulties are more likely to receive the scarce resources of therapy than those with the more extreme disorders (Herbert, 1998).

Social learning theory

Social learning theorists suggest that children and adolescents with such potentially serious antisocial problems are deviant because, *inter alia*, their early social learning/conditioning is ineffective. Youngsters with oppositional, conduct and (later) delinquent disorders have a fundamental inability or unwillingness to adhere to the rules and codes of conduct prescribed by society at its various levels. Such failures may be related to the lapse of poorly learned controls, to the failure to learn these controls in the first place, or to the fact that the behavioural standards a child has absorbed do not coincide with the norms of that section of society that enacts and enforces the rules.

The socialization process is a slow, continuing process, involving countless 'lessons' from parents, siblings, peers and adults in authority over the child. One of the child's major acquisitions on the road to becoming a social being is the development of internal controls over behaviour – the internalization of standards of conduct and morality implied by the term 'conscience'. Put in behavioural terms, a series of actions might be considered to be internalized to the extent that their maintenance has become independent of external outcomes. Their reinforcing consequences are internally generated (e.g. the 'voice of conscience') without external rewards and punishments. Norm-abiding behaviour ultimately depends not merely on avoidance of externally imposed sanctions but, more importantly, on the avoidance of aversive stimulation (anxiety and guilt) which has its source within the individual. There is substantial agreement about the parenting conditions conducive to the acquisition of internalized rules (norms). Effective parenting involves:

➢ a rich supply of positive reinforcement for positive behaviour 'fuelled' by a strong attachment to a caregiver with whom a child can therefore identify;
➢ firm moral demands made by parents upon their offspring, the consistent use of sanctions and techniques of punishment that are psychological rather than physical (i.e. methods which signify or threaten withdrawal of approval);
➢ intensive use of induction methods – reasoning and explanations.

Aronfreed (1968) and Baumrind (1971), among others, have demonstrated in a series of developmental studies how parents may have a choice as to whether, and how much, they bring out the following pro-social attributes in their children:

➢ appropriate feelings of guilt for wrongdoing;
➢ resistance to temptation;
➢ social and moral responsibility;
➢ outgoing qualities;
➢ competence;
➢ friendliness;
➢ creativity;
➢ self-assertion;
➢ independent behaviour (within defined limits).

These are, admittedly, Western, and more specifically American, values and, according to social learning theory, their fostering depends upon a number of factors:

➢ the timing of sanctions for misconduct (particularly the skill of nipping forbidden behaviours in the bud);
➢ the explanations given for sanctions (rewards and punishments);
➢ being firm and unbending at times;
➢ being tough as well as lovingly tender and flexible at others;
➢ knowing when to move from one modality to the other.

The so-called 'authoritative parent' (as opposed to the laissez-faire parent, who fails to set behavioural limits, or the authoritarian parent, who harshly prescribes rigid limits), according to Baumrind's research, demonstrates these qualities by setting appropriate, fair and firm rules. Here, then, are useful therapeutic goals or targets to discuss and negotiate with parents when planning 'remedial' and preventive behavioural programmes for children and adolescents.

A variety of economic, social and family conditions may preclude the operation of these facilitative factors in the lives of some children. Disharmonious home backgrounds, the breakdown of discipline, parental loss and broken homes are but a few of the variables that are linked aetiologically to conduct disorders. Maltreatment and witnessing parental aggression during early childhood are also predictive of children developing conduct disorders.

Development of antisocial disruptive disorders

There seems to be a typical developmental progression in which children start to show oppositional and confrontational behaviour early in life (usually between the ages of three and eight) and then gradually progress into increasingly severe patterns of antisocial behaviour. Although most children who display the most worrying conduct problems begin by manifesting somewhat less disruptive oppositional behaviours, a large number of those with the less challenging (oppositional) symptoms do not go on to the more severe conduct and delinquent problems. This is why a 'pyramid' with a large base and a smaller peak is used to illustrate this asymmetrical relationship – see Figure 2.

Most children who move on to display the more extreme types of conduct problem do not change the activities in their antisocial repertoire, but instead add to them. That is to say, most children with the more severe activities at the top of the pyramid continue to show conduct problems from the lower levels as well. Conduct problems appearing before adolescence are usually referred to as childhood-onset conduct disorders. Boys revealing childhood-onset conduct problems are more aggressive and have more neuropsychological deficits than boys with the adolescent-limited pattern. It would seem from these longitudinal findings that onset in childhood represents a much more serious pattern of dysfunction, whereas the adolescent-limited pattern may be better considered an exaggeration of the normal developmental process. Aggression is a good example of a worrying continuity of behaviour (from as early as three years of age) through to adulthood. We are talking of *extreme* antisocial, aggressive activity observed at that early stage (see Frick, 1987).

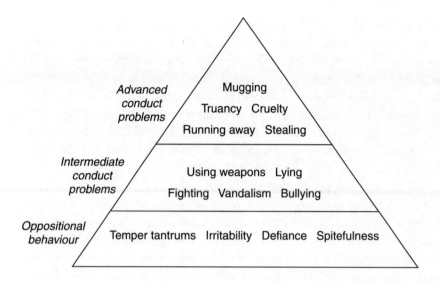

Figure 2. A visual heuristic describing the developmental progression of conduct problems. Problems at the lower levels of the pyramid tend to emerge earlier in development and are predictive of the emergence of more severe problems at the upper levels of the pyramid later in development (although of course many of those with oppositional behaviour do not go on to the more severe conduct and delinquent problems). (Adapted from Frick, 1987.)

Continuity of antisocial behaviour

There seem to be certain sub-groups of children with conduct disorders who show more persistent patterns of antisocial behaviour than others. One factor, as we have seen, is the age of onset. Other indicators of continuity include:

➤ the number of coexisting conduct problems;
➤ the presence of multiple types of conduct problems;
➤ the youngster having lower intelligence;
➤ the youngster having a parent with an antisocial disorder;
➤ the presence of attention deficit hyperactivity disorder (ADHD – the most recent diagnostic label for children presenting with significant problems with attention, impulse control and overactivity).

Children with ADHD are a heterogeneous population who display considerable variation in the degree of their symptoms, the pervasiveness across situations of these problems, and the extent to which other disorders occur in association with it. The disorder represents one of the most common reasons why children are referred to mental health practitioners and so is one of the most prevalent childhood psychiatric disorders.

Although conduct problems can create misery for everyone concerned with the younger child, the disturbance can often be contained within the home or classroom – although often at great cost. As children grow older, those problems that involve a persistent defiance of authority, together with a refusal or inability to show self-restraint, become more serious in their implications. They extend more and more beyond the confines of the child's life at home and school. The reverberations of the child's misdemeanours may eventually lead not only to the risk of being labelled 'conduct disordered', but also of earning the designation 'juvenile delinquent' if the child infringes the law, is apprehended and found guilty.

Retrospective studies suggest that most antisocial adults have childhood histories of antisocial behaviour. Estimates from prospective studies suggest that around 40 per cent of children with conduct disorders will exhibit antisocial personality disorder as adults. This means, however, that over half the children with conduct disorders will not show antisocial disorders as adults. The need for effective preventive and remedial programmes for children and parents is obvious, and fortunately they are now available (see Part III and Further reading).

Delinquent behaviour

Delinquency is perhaps the most noteworthy of all adolescent activities, reaching a peak at 15 years for boys and 14 years for girls. The term 'juvenile delinquent' is an administrative term, not a clinical diagnosis. It is clear from self-reports of delinquent-type activity that large numbers of young people engage in delinquent acts (e.g. petty theft and vandalism) for several years before they receive a police caution or are found guilty. Such activities tend to be transitory. By their twenties, most of the former offenders have gradually become broadly law-abiding members of the community. However, there is a small but hard core of adolescents who habitually break the law. Among these recidivists are the most dangerous and intractable offenders who pass through the revolving doors of the social services, justice and penal systems.

Bullying

Clinical observations of children and adolescents who exert continuing and extreme intimidation (including physical assaults) towards parents indicate that the majority of such families have some disturbance in the authority structure within the family. These children may develop a grandiose sense of self, feel omnipotent, and expect everyone to respond to them accordingly. It is suggested that they are seeking some kind of structure in a family environment which lacks boundaries and does not set limits. But they are not capable of providing those boundaries for themselves in any rational manner. The outcome is insecurity and a series of explosive responses to situations for which no prior family rules exist about making compromises and inhibiting aggression.

The intimidation described above is often directed at other children. Guerin and Hennessy (2001) have summarized the literature on bullying. A number of characteristics have been identified as common among both bullies and their victims and these include poor school performance and lower than average popularity. They are distinguished by their strong aggressive tendencies and weak control over these tendencies. They have a need to dominate. Family factors such as discipline and some patterns of family relationships have been associated with bullying.

Parental morale: learned helplessness

The frequency of critical messages conveyed to the parents of problem children from many sources (personal and professional) about their shortcomings tends to lower their morale and sap their self-confidence. Qualitative analyses (Webster-Stratton and Herbert, 1994) of parents' interviews indicated that the process of parenting a child with conduct disorders involved four phases:

➢ 'treading water' (hoping they'll outgrow the problem);
➢ recognition (reluctantly admitting the seriousness of the problem);
➢ searching for reasons (attributions);
➢ and, eventually, learned helplessness.

The cornerstone of the learned helplessness hypothesis is that people who undergo experiences over which they have no control often develop certain motivational, cognitive and emotional deficits, frequently ending in depression. The process of learned helplessness for these parents is characterized by a transition from self-blame to a desperate attempt to understand and cope, followed by a stage of giving up.

Causation

Conduct disorders represent the most intensively studied of all forms of childhood psychopathology. However, there is still great debate over how the accumulated facts should be interpreted. Why do antisocial trajectories develop? Why do they broaden and deepen with development in some children yet taper off in others? And why are they so difficult to deflect once stabilized? One of the factors contributing to the delinquency of many young people is their inability to cope with conflict with authority figures. Setting limits is a very real issue in the child's second year of life, although the foundations for good disciplinary practices should have been laid down much earlier. Notions of right and wrong, a code of behaviour, a set of attitudes and values, the ability to see the other person's point of view – all of these basic qualities which make an individual into a socialized personality – are nurtured in the first instance by parents.

Debates about advanced conduct disorder, specially when associated with horrific and apparently mindless acts, tends to be polarized into whether the perpetrator is 'mad' or 'bad'. The terms conduct disorder and delinquency suggest moral judgements and the suggestion is that offenders use less mature moral reasoning than non-offenders or, in the case of psychopaths, are devoid of conscience. Research indicates that there is some evidence to support this view, but it is inconclusive (Herbert, 1987, 1998).

Part III: Assessment and intervention

Behavioural assessment and formulation of the problem(s)

A rigorous assessment is the *sine qua non* of effective behavioural treatment. In summary, it requires measures of behavioural, cognitive and physiological responses as well as a determination of the developmental, social and cultural context within which the problems occur. The strategy is to begin with a broad-based assessment of the child and environment (e.g. family, school, peers) and then to obtain information regarding specific stimulus features, response modes, antecedents and consequences, severity, duration, and pervasiveness of the particular problem(s). The assessment utilizes a multi-method, problem-solving approach to obtain as complete a picture of the child and the family as possible. A formulation of the client's problem that bridges the assessment and the treatment plan is arrived at by several stages, summarized by the mnemonic ASPIRE (Sutton and Herbert, 1992).

Stage 1: Assessment (AS)
➢ Focusing on the 'what?' question – 'what is/are the problem(s)?'
➢ Focusing on the 'which?' question – 'which of the problems are to be addressed and in what order?'
➢ Focusing on the 'why?' question – 'why have the problems arisen?'

Stage 2: Planning (P)
➢ Focusing on the 'how?' question – 'how are we (practitioner and client together) going to address the problems?'

Stage 3: Implementation of the intervention (I)
➢ This refers to the initiation of an individual or group cognitive-behavioural programme.

Stage 4: Rigorous evaluation (RE)
➢ This refers to the assessment of change, monitoring the progress of the programme from beginning to end.

Stage 1: Assessment (AS)

The 'what', 'which' and 'why' questions are directed towards the precise identification of the antecedent, consequent and symbolic conditions (thoughts, feelings and beliefs) which control the targeted behaviour problems.

A   stands for *antecedent* events;
B   stands for *behaviours* – the target behaviours or interactions – and also for *beliefs* – the patient's (perhaps parent's) perception or interpretation of what is happening;
C   stands for the *consequences* that flow from these behaviours, interactions and beliefs.

This linear analysis is elaborated into a recursive sequence such that Cs become As, which generate new Cs, and thus ramify to affect the actions of others in the vicinity of the main protagonists (say, mother and child). The main assessment tasks are twofold: identifying particular problems and then looking at the variables associated with them.

Identifying target problems

The importance of a developmental context for (say) a child's fearfulness or aggressiveness cannot be overemphasized. The question arises from the essential normality of these emotions – they are universal responses to a wide range of life events and normal adaptations to particular environmental circumstances, and are functional in the sense of having positive survival and reward value. The parameters that separate behaviours defined as problematic from the aggression and antisocial behaviour manifested by all children at one time or another are their rate and intensity. Their persistence and pervasiveness, and the sheer number of problems with which they are associated, are also important diagnostic criteria. Their implications for the individual's well-being and 'effective' functioning provide a further diagnostic guideline for the therapist. The meaning of the problems for the child – the sense made of them, the payoff they provide – and indeed for the family constitute a vital element of the overall assessment.

Identifying controlling variables

In identifying controlling variables, two categories are generally considered:

➢   current environmental variables (antecedent and consequent events);
➢   organismic variables.

The contemporary causes of problem behaviour may exist in the client's environment or in his or her own thoughts, feelings, or bodily processes (organismic variables), and they may exert their influence in several ways: as eliciting or discriminative antecedent stimuli, or as outcomes (consequences) of a reinforcing kind.

Organismic variables include individual differences such as age, cognitive structures and past learning. Behaviour therapists tend to adopt a trans-actional position – the view that behaviour results from an interaction of the current situation and individual differences of a biological and psychosocial nature. The active and powerful influence of children on their parents' behaviour and choices is acknowledged (e.g. Herbert, 1998). A two-way 'traffic' is a feature of parent–child interactions and relationships.

The term 'life structure' is used to describe the interface between the internal and external worlds of the individual and to reflect the current social and psychological reality of the child's existence, the transition and change in his or her family life, as well as regrets and attitudes about his or her life. This moves the assessment on from a consideration of current antecedent influ-ences to an inquiry into distal (historical) precursors or antecedents to the problematic situation.

The identification of the current problem and its contemporary antecedents and consequences may be assisted by information about the client's past (e.g. attachments, health, 'reinforcement history' of rewards and punishments , attitudes and life events). But the information is gathered primarily as a source of clues to contemporary conditions that influence the elicitation and maintenance of symptoms rather than as a primary treatment objective in itself. The behaviour therapist places most emphasis on providing the patient with new learning experiences.

Stage 2: Planning (P)

The treatment plan and the tactical specification of methods/techniques for bringing about change – the 'how' question – generally flow from the assess-ment of the determinants or causes of the problems. In an ideal world, this formulation would inform the choice of therapeutic strategy or some broader-based community intervention. Only too often, however, the assessment data, like the occupants of Procrustes' bed, are made to fit the favoured therapeutic model. (There is often an implied, but erroneous, assumption that a particular approach can be applied to all problems.)

One of the strengths of behavioural approaches (the rigorous evaluation, stage 4 in the ASPIRE process) is that the specificity of goal-setting and the requirement to monitor change allow the therapist to judge fairly early on whether the programme is on the right track or not.

Stage 3: Implementation of the intervention

With all interventions, there are several ethical imperatives. The overall principles governing the choice of treatment should be those of alleviating distress, enhancing personal and social performance and, with it, quality of life. Such benefits should endure beyond the immediacies of the treatment process; and treatment should always be used within an overall planned programme of management. Young people may be limited in their understanding of a treatment or its implications and consequently unable to give full consent. It may, nevertheless, still be necessary to use a behavioural treatment; if so, it is essential that it is applied in such a way as to take the special needs of children into account. In evaluating the acceptability of a behavioural method or goal, the current social and professional consensus, taken in conjunction with the legitimately held values and beliefs of the client, should be considered in relation to the seriousness of the disturbance and its repercussions for the young person and for society.

Stage 4: Rigorous evaluation

The present-day demands in the health, and social and educational services for evidence-based approaches to one's work, and objective accounts of outcomes, makes a rigorous evaluation of therapeutic programmes a necessity. It should, in any event, be an ethical imperative for practitioners.

Choice of methods

There is space in this book for the description of only a limited selection of methods. Clearly, there is an urgent need to develop and evaluate standardized therapeutic programmes that can be distributed widely for purposes of training practitioners who in turn train parents, who in turn (hopefully) train their children.

The important question guiding the treatment is: how does this treatment achieve change? Ideally, treatment directly addresses the major processes involved in the development of the problem. I wish to claim that this is the case for behaviour therapy, behavioural family therapy and behavioural parent training, in dealing with antisocial conduct and delinquent disorders. All these approaches derive from social learning theory (at the strategic level) and cognitive-behavioural techniques (at the tactical level) (see Herbert, 2001).

Behaviour modification to cognitive-behaviour therapy

Operant methods (behaviour modification) using reinforcement of desired behaviour in the classroom and home have been repeatedly demonstrated to contribute to beneficial changes – albeit usually short term and situation specific – with disruptive behaviour, aggression, poor cooperation with peers and poor school attendance (e.g. Goldstein, 1995; Patterson, 1982).

At least three levels of intervention need to be implemented in concert in order to meet long-term goals (Evans, 1989):

➤ altering the immediate consequences of the undesirable behaviour and/ or beliefs;
➤ reducing the probability of the behaviour or beliefs by rearranging the environment (e.g. aggressive child behaviour provoked by parental mismanagement);
➤ facilitating (teaching, reinforcing, shaping) the emergence of alternative skills and attitudes (e.g. parenting skills groups).

At its simplest level (the first point above), the basic learning tasks commonly encountered in child therapy are: the acquisition of a desired response in which the individual is deficient; the reduction or elimination of an unwanted response in the child's repertoire; and the exchange of one response for another (e.g. social approach behaviour in place of excessively shy withdrawal). All of these goals and the treatment methods to which they give rise may be served by four major types of learning: operant and classical conditioning; observational and cognitive learning.

Behaviourists, the first 'behaviour modifiers', reacting in the 1950s and early 1960s to the subjectivism of psychoanalysis, sought a positivist approach to therapy and training for severely handicapped and disturbed children. It involved the systematic application of response-contingent (operant) principles of learning (operant behaviour being shaped and maintained by its positive or negative consequences) to the problem of autistic and mentally handicapped patients. Practitioners analysed the functional relationship between precisely defined observations of a targeted behaviour and its consequences.

A growing appreciation of the critical role of cognitive processes in childhood learning (see Herbert, 1998) led to a reappraisal by behaviour therapists (some reluctantly) of the significance of private events, and the cognitive mediation of problem behaviour. Thus, we arrive, in the 1980s and 1990s, at propositions underpinning what came to be known as cognitive-behavioural therapy, namely that thoughts, feelings and behaviour are causally related, and that children and adolescents can be taught to eliminate maladaptive behaviours by challenging their irrational beliefs and faulty logic. Cognitive-behaviour therapy (CBT) techniques include Socratic questioning, persuasion, challenging, debate, hypothesizing, cognitive restructuring, verbal self-instruction and internal dialogues, while the behavioural techniques include operant procedures, desensitization, exposure training, social skills training, role play, behaviour rehearsal, modelling, exercise, redefinition and self-monitoring.

Behavioural family therapy

Behavioural family work is based on the rationale that many of the problematic behaviours of childhood are developed and sustained in the home by dysfunctional parent–child (and other intra-familial) interactions. These maladaptive interactions, in turn, have their origins on both sides of the parent–child equation, in a host of biological, social and psychological factors. In simplistic terms, parents influence children's pro-social behaviour through positively reinforcing consequences such as attention, praise and the delivery of rewards (e.g. treats, privileges and time with a parent). The theory suggests that children's uncooperative or antisocial acts can be reinforced inadvertently by parents' attention to them, or by their attempts to placate the child. As a result, it is often necessary for parents to offer brief, mild punishments for such behaviour. A procedure known as 'time out' was developed as one such strategy. In time out, a parent removes a child for a brief period of time from any reinforcement or attention following an undesired behaviour.

As research on the interactions of families progressed, it became clear that there was an additional critical feature of interactions in these families, namely, coercion. In a coercive interaction, the aversive behaviour of each person is terminated or reduced in frequency by the aversive behaviour of the other person, but the long-term effect is to increase the likelihood that the original aversive behaviour will occur again. For example, a parent orders a child to do something and the child whines and complains. If the parent stops insisting that the child do what was asked, the child's whining is negatively reinforced by the removal of the parent's demand. The parent's behaviour of dropping the demand is also negatively reinforced when the child stops whining. Thus, both the whining and the removal of parents' demands are more likely to be repeated in future interactions.

If left unchanged, these coercive patterns of interaction continue into school life and adulthood. In the most general terms, social learning theorists suggest that the very processes of learning that help children adapt to life can, under certain circumstances, contribute to their maladaptive behaviour. An immature child who learns by imitating an adult is not necessarily to know when it is deviant behaviour that is being modelled. A parent may unwittingly reinforce deviant behaviour and extinguish pro-social actions.

If it is accepted that many deviant behaviours of childhood and adulthood are acquired as a function of faulty learning processes or as a result of the absence of appropriate training (for whatever reason), then there is a case for arguing that problems can most effectively be modified (and, indeed, prevented), when and where they occur, by changing the social lessons the child receives or the reinforcing contingencies supplied by social agents, or by building in the training that failed to take place earlier.

Behavioural parent training

The core of behavioural family intervention is training parents in child management strategies (i.e. disciplinary methods) based upon social learning and developmental principles. Behavioural work starts from a clear objective of producing planned, goal-directed change. Behaviour therapy based on the one-to-one (dyadic) or behavioural family therapy (systemic) model tends to take place in the clinic. Behavioural training based on the triadic or behavioural consultation model (using significant caregivers or teachers as mediators of change) generally takes place in the home, or is geared to the home. It may be located in the school or, when it involves group work, in a community centre. Although the distinction between treatment and training is at times indistinct, the treatment model is most appropriate to the emotional disorders of childhood (e.g. fears and phobias), and the training model to the longer-term problems (e.g. antisocial behaviour and pervasive developmental disorders).

At its simplest level there are certain basic learning tasks that are commonly encountered in child therapy:

➢ the acquisition (learning) of a desired response in which the individual is deficient (e.g. compliance to medication regimes, self-esteem, self-control, fluent speech, social or academic skills);

➢ the reduction or elimination (unlearning) of an unwanted response in the child's repertoire (e.g. self-deprecatory self-talk, aggression, stealing, facial tics, phobic anxiety, compulsive eating) or the exchange of one response for another (e.g. self-assertion in place of shy withdrawal).

Training programmes address themselves to the fact that parents of children with behaviour problems tend to flounder because they issue so many commands, provide attention following deviant behaviour, are unlikely to perceive deviant behaviour as deviant, get frequently embroiled in extended coercive hostile interchanges, give vague commands and are generally ineffectual in bringing their children's deviant behaviour to a halt. Parents of children with conduct problems give more negative commands than parents of non-challenging youngsters. Those with reasonably obedient children give more so-called alpha commands. These effective methods are characterized by being specific and direct, being given one at a time and being followed by a wait of five seconds. Parents can be taught to use these, rather than ineffective beta commands – chain commands, vague commands, question commands, 'let's' commands, and commands followed by a rationale or verbalization.

Parent training programmes emphasize methods designed to reduce confrontations and antagonistic interactions among the family members, to increase the effectiveness of positive interactions and moderate the intensity of parental punishment. Parents are encouraged and guided to increase their positive interactions with their children through the use of play and other activities. They are encouraged to reinforce their children's appropriate behaviour with praise, encouragement and other rewards. They are helped to avoid giving unnecessary commands, increasing the clarity of the limits they set, and increasing the consistency with which they follow through on their limits. To do this they are guided in the implementation of brief, mild, non-violent sanctions such as judicious ignoring, time out and loss of privileges. They are provided with the means of understanding and analysing problematic behaviour, and ways of negotiating and problem solving their way out of previously corrosive, confrontational conflict situations. They are also encouraged to monitor their children effectively, and to engage in effective communication.

Evaluation

Properly designed studies showing the effectiveness of this approach (see Further reading) are more numerous than those supporting any other approach for treating children and families. In the short term, individually based behavioural parent training (BPT) spanning 10–20 sessions is more effective than no treatment or less clearly focused family interventions. Group-based BPT programmes also have a good record (see Herbert and Wookey, 1998).

Specific studies (see review by Webster-Stratton in Webster-Stratton and Herbert, 1994) have demonstrated that:

➤ short-term treatment leads to significant changes in parents' and children's behaviour and in parental perceptions of child adjustment;
➤ parents can be successful in reducing children's level of aggression by 20–60 per cent;
➤ there is a generalization of improvements from clinic to the home over follow-up periods of up to four years;
➤ there is a generalization to untreated child behaviours;
➤ there are high parental ratings of acceptability and consumer satisfaction.

Working with parents

Researchers have evaluated the effectiveness of adding a number of components to the parenting skills interventions besides child management training. These issues are addressed by Webster-Stratton and Herbert (1994) in their discussion of the 'collaborative approach' to therapy. It is important:

> ➤ to build a supportive relationship with the parents – this is often achieved through appropriate use of self-disclosure, humour and optimism, as well as actively advocating for parents (such as at the child's school), as appropriate;
> ➤ to empower parents, through reinforcing and validating their insights, helping them to modify thoughts of their powerlessness, promoting self-empowerment and building family and group supports;
> ➤ to teach by persuading, explaining, suggesting, adapting, giving assignments, reviewing, summarizing, ensuring generalization, using videotape examples and role playing;
> ➤ to interpret or 'translate' the cognitive, behavioural and developmental concepts into words that the parents can understand and apply – this includes the use of analogies and metaphors, reframing (cognitive restructuring) and making connections between the parents' own childhood or other life experiences and those of the child;
> ➤ to lead and challenge, including setting limits (especially in groups), pacing the sessions and dealing with resistance;
> ➤ to 'prophesy' – anticipating problems and setbacks, predicting parent resistance to change, and predicting positive change and success.

This partnership between clients and therapist has the effect of giving back dignity, respect and self-control to parents who are often seeking help for their children's problems at a vulnerable time of low self-confidence and intense feelings of guilt and self-blame. It is our hypothesis that a collaborative model, which gives parents responsibility for developing solutions (alongside the therapist), is more likely to increase parents' confidence and perceived self-efficacy than are approaches that do not hold them responsible for solutions. Parents who are self-efficacious tend to persist at tasks in the face of difficulties until success is achieved. They are less likely to show debilitating effects of stress. Moreover, there is some evidence that the collaborative process has the multiple advantages of reducing attrition rates, increasing motivation and commitment, and giving both parents and the therapist a stake in the outcome of the intervention efforts (Herbert, 1998; Herbert and Wookey, 1998). See Part IV for an example of a BPT programme. It is a group counselling and applied social learning course for parents with challenging children aged three to eight years but can be adapted to use with school-age children and adolescents, as the author has established, working with foster parents and the youngsters in their care.

Multimodal interventions

Behavioural methods for delinquents are usually embedded within multi-modal interventions. The treatment package might involve communication training, feedback, positive interruptions, problem-solving and decision-making skills, providing rationales, happy talk, positive requests, non-blaming communication, negotiation skills-training, family games and a variety of behavioural methods. Contracts are drawn up defining goals and mutual obligations (see Part IV).

While there are encouraging demonstrations of short-term changes from programmes like these on a variety of quantitative and qualitative outcome measures, there is less room for optimism about the longer term and about (in the case of delinquent youngsters) significant generalization to offending behaviour.

Cognitive-behaviour therapy (direct work with adolescents)

The issue of parent involvement gives rise to a conceptual boundary problem. At what stage in childhood-onset conduct disorders does the practitioner shift the therapy paradigm from the so-called triadic model, which involves caregivers as primary mediators of change (e.g. in successful parenting skills programmes), to one that more appropriately deals with an individual in his/her own right? Cognitive-behavioural approaches to the study of aggression have come to the fore in recent years, pointing to the possibility that attributional biases (beliefs, attitudes, theories) may make some individual children and adolescents more vulnerable to provocation and more inclined to perceive aggressive responses as a means of dealing with conflicts. Children and adolescents with these disorders display a range of social-cognitive distortions and ineffectual problem-solving skills (Frick, 1987). They tend, for example, to have difficulty anticipating the consequences of their behaviour, and under-perceive their responsibility in the early stages of conflict. They lack empathy and insight.

These distortions are addressed in individual or group work with adolescents in their own right, and are discussed in parent management skills groups (see Herbert and Wookey, 1998; Webster-Stratton and Herbert, 1994). There are anger-management programmes designed specifically for adolescents. Among the best known multimodal cognitive-behavioural programmes is aggression replacement training (ART) (Herbert, 1987), which includes three main approaches to changing behaviour: structured social skills learning (social skills and social problem solving), anger control training and moral education. Outcome studies indicate that the programmes have led to improved skills, improved self-control and more acceptable institutional behaviour.

Ecological interventions

Structural causes that undermine parenting and family life, such as poor housing, inner-city deprivation and alienation, contribute to the development of conduct disorders. Other risk factors, more within the remit of the clinical, educational and social work professions' remedial/preventive roles, have to do with poor family support, the absence of a positive school climate and failures of community socialization. Such broad-spectrum problems require a broad-band ecological approach. They are delivered across multiple domains of functioning and across multiple social settings. They are designed to promote competence and reduce risk of early-onset conduct disorder, substance abuse and school failure. The programme makes use of behavioural methods in the home and classroom. There is a recognition that narrowly focused interventions fail for a significant number of families with a child with conduct disorder.

Part IV: Examples of interventions in practice

A collaborative cognitive-behavioural approach

The course begins with a home visit to introduce ourselves, explain the nature of the programme, make a working contract, arrange for some baseline measures, observe the child's interactions with the family, discuss practical arrangements and leave a handout describing what lies ahead.

Each session lasts two hours, with a 20-minute refreshment and socializing break. Given the continuities from toddlerhood to adolescence, these preventive groups are critical. They are, as I have said, adaptable for parents of teenagers. Groups should not number more than 12 parents, otherwise discussion and debate become difficult. A community centre is an excellent venue for meetings as they are informal and have tea-making facilities.

Session 1: Group induction

Introductions/welcoming

➢ Personal introductions.
➢ Purpose of groups and ground rules (aims and expectations) discussed.
➢ Ground rules agreed.
➢ Parents show photographs of their children with a brief description (name, age, siblings etc.).

Sharing problems ('I'm not the only one')

➢ Parents describe their difficulties with their children (written up on a flip chart).
➢ Video and/or brief case illustration of a challenging child/adolescent discussed and debated.

Describing and tackling behaviour problems

➢ Defining behavioural/emotional problems.
➢ How to avoid vague language ('fuzzies') in observing and describing behaviour (flip chart examples followed by discussion).
➢ How to tease out 'ABC of behaviour' sequences (e.g., for temper tantrums).

Parents' needs

➢ Parents identify their ideas on parents' needs (flip chart).
➢ Why needy parents find it difficult to attend to needy children and teenagers.
➢ Discussion and debate.

Pre-training (baseline) questionnaires

➢ These are filled in along with the weekly evaluation form.

Homework tasks

➢ Record (track) a target behaviour (antisocial and problematic) on pro formas provided.

Session 2: Children's (adolescents') needs

Preliminaries

➢ Refreshments.
➢ Welcome.
➢ Forms collected.

Précis

➢ Highlighting main points from previous session.
➢ Discussion of homework – participants' record-keeping (to be a regular feature each session).

Children's needs

➢ What are they?
➢ Brainstorming – participants' ideas written up on the flip chart.
➢ Compare parents' needs (from last week) with adolescents' needs and discuss results.
➢ Look at links between the generations.

A child's/ teenager's perspective

➤ Seeing the world from a youngster's point of view (suitable video or role play).
➤ The child/teenager as 'learner' and 'problem solver' (cartoon/quotations).
➤ Developmental tasks (handouts; developmental milestones charts given out).
➤ Discussion and debate of implications for child and parents of their interacting at their respective stages of development.

Parental attention

➤ Positive attention and its importance.
➤ Finding and creating 'special/quality' time and suitable shared activities.
➤ Negative attention (reinforcing unwanted behaviour).
➤ Differential attention.
➤ Shared activities as special/quality time.
➤ Discussion.

Summarizing and highlighting

➤ Provide summaries at convenient intervals with emphasis on important points.

Homework

➤ Find at least 15 minutes daily for 'special' time with your child (e.g. conversation with an adolescent).
➤ Record interesting reactions – yours and hers/his (record forms provided).

Evaluation

➤ Forms filled in and collected.

Session 3: Play as 'special' quality time

Preliminaries

➤ Welcome.
➤ Resumé.
➤ Collect homework.

Homework feedback

➢ Individual and group discussion.
➢ Prompts (How did you spend your special time with your child/ teen-ager? Were there any difficulties? Did you enjoy the time? Did she/he? If not, why not?)

Parents' experience of play and adolescent leisure activities

➢ Memories of childhood play/adolescent activities (flip chart).
➢ Brainstorm functions and meaning of play/leisure activities.

Exposition on play/leisure activities (video)

➢ Role play (illustrate intrusive joining in; helpful interactions).
➢ Demonstrate codes for different kinds of interaction.
➢ Role-play interacting with your child to her/his advantage.

Homework task

➢ Interact with your child for about 30 minutes each day.
➢ Keep a record of what happens.

Evaluation

Session 4: Effective praise

Preliminaries

➢ Welcome.
➢ Resumé .
➢ Collect homework.

Homework feedback

➢ Individual and group feedback.
➢ Discussion prompts key questions:
  • How many participants found time to play/interact as suggested?
  • What factors affected the quantity/quality of the play periods (e.g. fatigue, lack of time, telephone calls, child's attitude, feelings about this task.) Discuss ways of handling these issues.

- What effect did the play/conversation/other interactive sessions have on the parent–child relationship?
- Play can also involve joining a parent in, say, baking, cleaning the car, sporting activities, eating out. These can be quality time activities.

The ABC analysis

➢ Exposition/video vignette/role play to illustrate the ABC of behaviour and beliefs (attributions).
➢ The good behaviour rule.
➢ Parents' examples of ABC sequences at home (child's behaviour/their beliefs about it; their behaviour/the young person's likely beliefs and attributions).
➢ How to encourage desired behaviour.

How and what to praise

➢ Brainstorm these questions (using flip chart).
➢ Being specific (labelling praise).
➢ Discussion and debate.

Suggestive praise

➢ Examples of ways to praise and when.
➢ Schedules of reinforcement.
➢ Praise as reinforcement.

Homework tasks

➢ Praise your child/teenager for behaviours you like to see.
➢ Keep a record of some instances. (How did you feel? How did she/he react?)

Brief recap

Evaluation forms

➢ Filled in and collected.

Session 5: Tangible and social rewards

Preliminaries

➤ Welcome.
➤ Resumé.
➤ Collect homework.

Homework feedback

➤ Individual and group feedback.
➤ Discussion (How often and in what situations did parents praise their children? In what ways did they do this?)

Rewards and incentives

➤ Rewards, incentives and privileges.
➤ Parents' experiences in childhood/adolescence of receiving social and tangible rewards.
➤ Ways of rewarding desired behaviour.
➤ Discussion and role play.

Symbolic rewards

➤ Rationale.
➤ Illustration of imaginative reward/sticker charts (points for older children).
➤ Brainstorm of ideas for making charts.

Homework task

➤ Design a behaviour (reward) chart or points system with your child.
➤ Try it out.

Evaluation and handouts

Session 6: It's as simple as ABC
(where B stands for beliefs and behaviour)

Preliminaries

➤ Welcome.
➤ Resumé.
➤ Collect homework.

Homework feedback

➤ View charts or points log the parents have made.
➤ What were the child's responses?
➤ In what situations were they used?

Beliefs, thoughts and feelings

➤ Explore links between thoughts, feelings and behaviour.
➤ Brief exposition on the 'stories' people tell themselves, about themselves and their children.
➤ How they affect behaviour and relationships.
➤ Group members describe thoughts and feelings they have linked to their parenting activities and methods.
➤ Notion of 'learned helplessness' is explored.
➤ The influence of culture and myth on the so-called 'perfect' parent.
➤ Acknowledgement that parenting is a hard and complex job.
➤ How helpful or undermining is the advice/attitudes of friends, relatives and neighbours?

The ABC of behaviour

➤ The ABC sequence is explained and explored – also role played.
➤ Its role in learning pro-social and antisocial behaviour.
➤ Importance of antecedent/setting events (triggers to actions).

'Pay-offs'

➤ The function of consequences (pay-offs).

Homework tasks

➤ Parents apply the ABC model at home with pro formas provided.

Evaluation and handouts

Session 7: Discipline

Preliminaries

> ➤ Welcome.
> ➤ Resumé.
> ➤ Collect homework

Homework feedback

> ➤ Individual and group feedback.
> ➤ Discuss any difficulties participants had with last week's task.
> ➤ Examine records.

Discipline

> ➤ What is discipline? (Unnecessary equation with punishment only, rather than positive guidance.)
> ➤ Positive parenting.
> ➤ Why is discipline important?
> ➤ How is it implemented?

Rules, roles and limits

> ➤ Why rules?
> ➤ Who rules?
> ➤ Setting limits.
> ➤ Where should they be drawn?
> ➤ Firm or soft limits?
> ➤ Giving reasons for rules.
> ➤ Negotiating rules.

Giving instructions and making requests

> ➤ What is the difference?
> ➤ How to give them.
> ➤ Parents look back to their childhood and/or adolescence and to their experience of rules, roles and limits, which is to say what their parents called 'discipline'.

Physical punishment

> ➤ Advantages and disadvantages (brainstorm/flip chart).
> ➤ Does smacking actually work on your child?

➤ The trouble with smacking.
➤ Risks – short and long term.
➤ The issue of authority in the family.
➤ Differences of opinion on discipline and other child-rearing issues within the family. (For teenagers, the question of verbal criticism, nagging and 'put downs'.)

Homework tasks

➤ Record instances where you were tempted to smack your child (put down your teenager), but used an alternative method.
➤ Record how you felt before, during and after the episode.
➤ How did your child react?
➤ Draw out the ABC of the incident to tell the group next week.

Evaluation and handouts

Sessions 8–11

Session 8

➤ Planned (judicious) ignoring.
➤ Time-out/grounding.
➤ Ethical imperatives (e.g. issues of personal choice for children).

Session 9

➤ Taking away rewards and privileges (response-cost).
➤ Problem-solving particular stressful situations (e.g. supermarkets, visiting).

Session 10

➤ Caring for yourself (stress management).
➤ Parents' charter/children's rights – keeping a balance.
➤ Relaxation exercises.
➤ Getting help (sources of help for financial/housing/personal difficulties).
➤ Endings (arrangements for further contacts/farewell party).

Session 11: Booster sessions, reunion and trouble shooting

- ➤ Reminders.
- ➤ Feedback.
- ➤ Reassurance re behavioural drift (slippage).
- ➤ Social (farewell party).

These methods are more fully described in a validated programme (see Herbert and Wookey, 1998).

Confrontation and conflict, negotiation skills and the use of family contracts

Psychologists have worked out ways of discussing risk-taking privileges and freedoms with adolescents, ways of reaching rational compromises and negotiating mutually satisfactory goals for family life. These are sometimes enshrined in family agreements or 'contracts'. It is particularly valuable to be able to speak directly and honestly to the teenager. Parents who have fostered a good relationship and honest lines of communication with their children are best placed to sensitize them to danger and strengthen their resolve not to overstep the bounds of reasonable behaviour and risk taking.

There is evidence that at times of crisis, when members of a family are seriously at loggerheads, angry and distressed, the negotiating process and the existence of a family contract provides an opportunity for a family to break through a vicious circle of hostility and unreason. The method is also helpful with the more mundane but trying confrontations that arise between parents and teenagers in the course of day-to-day living. They can also (incidentally) restore goodwill to strained marital/partnership relationships.

The point is that disharmony is seldom unilateral; it takes two or more to quarrel or disagree. The channels of communication – for a real meeting of minds – are rusty or non-existent. What passes for communication are often punitive messages: a surfeit of coercion, criticism and nagging (see Patterson, 1982). Kind and affectionate ('reinforcing') words and actions are notable for their absence! The give and take ('reciprocity') which is the essence of contented family life is minimal; thus it is not surprising to find little of the negotiation and compromise by which most families sort out the sometimes competing needs of their individual members. A lack of clear expectations about the rules and the individual roles that apply (for children and adults alike) within the family group makes for misunderstandings and heated disputes. In a nutshell: coercion reigns; cooperation has taken flight. The longer-term consequences can be serious. The absence of family cohesion has a marked and adverse effect on the psychological well-being of the individual.

If people genuinely wish to bring about change – and are prepared to examine critically their own actions – then there are 'therapeutic' elements to the very process of negotiating and drawing up a contract, which, together with the disciplines of implementing it, can put into reverse the corrosive features that undermine family life. These elements provide members with the opportunity to discuss their common objectives and values, to practise the give and take of compromise and, most important (perhaps), re-establish trust. A contract is a publicly endorsed, unambiguous and specific commitment to a future course of action; as such it tends to prove more binding, a better guarantee of compliance than more casual 'promises' ('I won't do it again Mum ... I promise') or ephemeral statements of intention such as New Year resolutions.

Before looking at the practicalities, let us briefly examine the credentials for this approach. Social psychology tells us that groups which exist for any length of time (and we can think here of the family group as a particular example) have a definite communication structure. For example, there tends to be consistency in the number of communications individuals receive and in the number (and content) of communications they initiate. There is a strong association between the frequency of communications ('in' and 'out') and the status of the individual in the group. One can imagine that powerless members of the family (say, teenagers) are allowed or able to say very little for themselves when 'put down' by a domineering father. It is important (in family contract work) to point out to clients how the actions of one individual are the signal (or 'cue') for the actions of the other, which in turn become cues for the reactions of the first. And cues are by definition 'carriers' of information; this transmission of information is the essence of communication. But what kind of messages do people give each other – not only in what they say (verbal cues) but what they do or the way in which they say things (non-verbal cues)? Sadly, they are often very negative, and sometimes destructive (see Patterson, 1982, for a discussion of coercive family interactions).

Agreements are not unnatural to most people. There is an element of exchange and bargaining in the undercurrents (and sometimes on the surface) of most personal relationships. Social relationships can be compared, up to a point, to economic bargains.

There seems to be a ratio of 'rewards' and 'costs' underlying these interactions. Those actions – words and deeds – carried out by one individual to the benefit of another are termed rewards, while detrimental activities which involve, say, hostility and insensitivity, and result in anxiety or embarrassment, are counted as costs. The loss or deprivation of rewards can also be seen as a cost. Thus the perpetual failure to praise and acknowledge children's little (or big) successes would be costly, and might affect their self-esteem over the years into adolescence.

The ratio of rewards to costs is called the 'outcome'. If the overall outcome is positive, it may be said to yield a 'profit'. Individuals have what is called a comparison level – a level of profit they have come to expect (or believe they deserve) from these relationships. Relationships break down when the 'debit' column over a long period heavily outweighs the 'credit' column, registering a chronic state of loss.

Contracting

This state of affairs was reflected in the Greens' relationship with their adolescent daughter, Amie – a family with parents and daughter at war. A behavioural counsellor began to 'unravel' their complaints and actions. Her suggestion of a contract came as a bit of a surprise to the Greens, but after a family consultation they agreed to it. The contract – following careful preparation – was a 'mutual endeavour' agreement between Mr and Mrs Green and Amie, based on the principle of reciprocity. Below is their contract.

CONTRACT between Mr and Mrs Green and Amie

Amie's parents would like her:

- to let them know about her movements when she goes out at night – Amie will let them know by telling them where she is and with whom, and letting them know when she'll be home;
- to be less moody – she won't go silent ('sulk') for hours on end when reprimanded or thwarted;
- to be more ready to say sorry – that is, she will apologize when she's been in the wrong;
- to show more concern about her school work (e.g. homework), and will put in at least an hour per night;
- to stop being so rude to her father (e.g. walking out when he gives her advice).

Amie would like her father and mother:

- to stop criticizing her friends all the time (i.e. stop calling them names and saying they're no good);
- to admit when they are in the wrong – that is, they will apologize when they have been in the wrong in their confrontations with her;

- to give her more pocket money (a sum agreed) and to review the amount every six months in the light of rising expenses and changing nature of her commitments.

All agree:

- that the terms of the contract will not be changed except by mutual discussion and agreement;
- that disputes will be settled by the witness (grandmother), whom all accept to be objective and fair-minded;
- that successful execution of the contract for a month will be rewarded by a family treat (first month: an outing to a posh, named restaurant);
- that failure to carry out individual terms of the contract will result in a fine on each occasion (an amount of *x* for Amie and *y* for Mr and Mrs Green, the money to go into a 'penalty box', kept by the grandmother, the proceeds of which to go to a charity of her choice).

Signed: Amie
            Mr Green
            Mrs Green
            Grandmother (witness)

The following elements of contracting are important to remember.

➤ Be very specific in spelling out the desired actions; avoid being vague (e.g. 'I wish he'd be more helpful'). Be concrete and specific (e.g. 'I wish he'd help me set and clear the table').

➤ Pay attention to the details of the privileges and conditions for both parties; they should be important as opposed to trivial, and make sense to the person involved.

➤ Encourage positive actions if parents wish their teenager to desist from certain actions and activities. (For example, if parents would like their teenager to stop being so critical and negative they should specify the change they wish to bring about by inviting him or her to accentuate the positive, the pleasant or praiseworthy. This would then have to be spelled out in terms of specific examples of behaviour – words and deeds.)

➤ Choose actions that are readily observable – so they can be monitored.

➤ Make it clear what incentives there are for keeping to the contract and what sanctions will be imposed for breaking the contract.

➤ It is not only the 'signed and sealed' contract that helps concentrate people's minds on their commitments. It is the process of sitting down as a family, the shared activities of discussing common goals, of settling differences and of treating one another with respect and dignity that have a healing and constructive part to play.

Resolving conflicts and settling differences

Conflict situations are those interpersonal situations in which the youth and authority figure (such as a parent or teacher) have opposing wishes or plans. The youth may want to buy a motorbike, but his mother wants him to purchase an old car because she thinks bikes are dangerous and will get him into bad company. Youngsters often make inappropriate responses to conflict situations (such as fighting, withdrawing, tantrums or destructive behaviour); a serious escalation of conflict may bring them into contact with clinics, court and other agencies.

Negotiation can sometimes defuse these situations and produce more acceptable consequences for both parties. There are two broad approaches to conflict resolution:

➤ arbitration or mediation of specific conflict;
➤ modification of the communication process.

Behavioural agreements are the most common form of arbitration. The therapist assumes the role of mediator or arbitrator and thus facilitates mutual agreements between opposing parties about reciprocal exchanges of specific behaviours and reinforcers. Verbal instructions, practice and feed-back are the major techniques used to modify communication process. The emphasis is placed on learning new adaptive behaviours, rather than eliminating problem behaviours, and the techniques are primarily educational rather than therapeutic.

The organizers of a UK Open University course ('Parents and Teenagers') suggest a step-by-step approach to settling differences of opinion between parents and adolescents. Let us take the example that parents often mention to practitioners: a clash with a teenage son who wishes to buy a motorbike against his mother's wishes. The following six steps might be suggested to the worried parent.

(1) Try to work out your attitudes and feelings about the situation before you approach your son. Completing this sentence can help you to clarify it in your mind:

➤ I feel ... (describe your feeling – angry, afraid, etc.)
➤ when he ... (describe the situation, e.g. talks about buying a motorbike)
➤ because ... (describe why you feel that way).

(2) Decide whether the particular situation is worth having all this bother for. List several reasons why the issue is worth raising, and why it may not be. Rate your reasons *** for very important, * for trivial. Do the reasons for tackling the issue outweigh the reasons against, or is it finely balanced? The example above might go like this:

➤ Reasons for talking to my son about the wisdom of buying a motorbike:
   He may be injured or killed (there is a high risk). ****
   He can't really afford it. **
   Motorbikes are associated with rather rough types.*

➤ Reasons against:
   There'll be another awful row between us.***
   He'll do as he pleases anyway.*
   He needs some transport and he certainly can't afford a car.**

(3) Decide on the spirit in which you will raise the matter. For example, 'I want to deal with it ...' (firmly, forcefully, mildly, etc.).

(4) Approach your teenager:

➤ Begin by telling him how you feel, and why (see step 1).
➤ Avoid expressing your feeling as criticisms or attacks which will make him defensive or aggressive.

(5) Listen to his reply and check your understanding of:

➤ his feelings about the situation;
➤ his reasons for them.

Say: 'You feel ... because ...' and see if you have his point of view clear in your mind.

(6) Work out a practical agreement/compromise, if you can. It may be difficult, sometimes impossible; but it is more likely that you'll find a solution if you acknowledge his feelings, explain yours, and discuss matters quietly and calmly, and with goodwill.

This particular example is a difficult one for parents to resolve because a compromise is not easy and also because of the risk involved. Parents are proud (even pleased) when young children are daring, even though they may feel worried (say) at the height of the tree climbed or the speed with which the bike is ridden. Teenagers will take risks; they are a necessary part of adolescent experimentation. But the risks are sometimes too high, and the judgement (and experience) of the adolescent too limited to allow parents to acquiesce in their activities.

Parents typically list the following risks that cause them worry:

➤ that their child will be in an accident;
➤ that their child will be killed;
➤ that their child will be assaulted or raped;
➤ that their child will get into a fight or get into trouble with authority (teachers, police);

➤ that their child will get a girl pregnant or will get pregnant, or get AIDS;
➤ that their child will harm him/herself, or harm someone else;
➤ that their child will try out and succumb to drugs;
➤ that their child will make the wrong choice of partner.

Training in problem-solving skills

Problem-solving skills provide parents and their adolescent children with a general coping strategy for a variety of difficult situations. They could help teenagers to deal more effectively with a variety of conflict situations, such as choosing between alternative courses of action, arriving at mutually acceptable decisions with parents, or developing cooperation with the peer group. The particular advantage of the problem-solving approach is that it teaches people how to think and work things out for themselves. There are four steps.

(1) General orientation

This is by way of an introductory scene-setting exercise – trying with the young person's help to gain some perspective about the nature of the problem, putting it into a context of why, when and how it occurs. It is important that the youngster should be able to recognize the problem and the 'danger' signs. The youngster might think back over the events that have given rise in the past to the problem situation. If this sheds no light on the difficulty parents can encourage their child to monitor future circumstances that prove problematic (e.g. a diary of events).

(2) Problem definition and formulation

Define all aspects of the problem as explicitly as possible, in concrete terms rather than in vague and abstract language. This helps to unravel what looks like a complicated problem and, perhaps, to simplify it.

Here is an example of an exasperated parent:

> I get angry with my son David. My muscles tense up. I want to lash out at him when he is cheeky. But what do I mean when I say he's cheeky? It's when I feel that my dignity is threatened, especially when my friends are present, or that my authority is demeaned. It's something about his manner, dumb insolence I call it, unfriendly. And then, eventually, I explode in a torrent of recrimination and abuse. Perhaps he also feels provoked by my manner. I must think about that.

Next, the salient features of the particular situation should be categorized in a way that identifies the main goals of those involved and the obstacles that get in the way of the fulfilment of these goals. For example, David's mother wishes to improve her relationship with her son (the goal), her interpretation of his motives and manner and possibly her own attitude towards him. This stage is a further clarification of what may be going wrong and why this should be so.

(3) Setting goals

Setting goals is at the centre of the attempt to solve problems; parents' help in this matter could be invaluable. A workable goal is an accomplishment that helps the individual manage problematic situations. The goal is achieved when the individual has acquired new skills, practised them, and actually used them to solve or manage the situation causing all the difficulties. This accomplishment is often referred to in counselling as the new (or preferred) scenario.

Here are some scenarios based on questions adolescents can usefully ask themselves:

Q   What would the problem situation be like if I could cope better?
A   I'd be able to talk to others without feeling awkward and tongue-tied; I would not spend so much time on my own.

Q   What changes would take place in my lifestyle?
A   I'd go out with a nice girl. I'd be more ambitious; take an interest.

Q   What would be happening that is not happening now?
A   I'd go to concerts, the cinema and plays instead of always moping in front of the television.

Scenarios and goals can help young adults in difficulty in four ways:

➢ They focus the person's attention and action. They provide a vision which offers hope and an outlet for concerted effort.
➢ They mobilize energy and help pull the worrier out of the inertia of helplessness and depression.
➢ They enhance the persistence needed for working at the problem.
➢ They motivate people to search for strategies to accomplish their goals.

If you can help adolescents to the point of defining goals, they are, in essence, on the first stage of 'recovery' – orientating them to face life rather than turning away from it, embracing optimism rather than resignation.

Goals should preferably be:

> specific, a necessity if they are to be converted into actions;
> measurable, that is, capable of providing feedback that change is occurring and, eventually, verifying that the objective has been accomplished;
> realistic, in the sense that the adolescent has the resources to achieve them; that external circumstances are not bound to thwart their accomplishment; that the goals are under the control (potentially) of the teenager; and the cost of obtaining them is not too high;
> pertinent to their problem and not simply a partial solution or even a diversionary move;
> the adolescent's own goals and not those he or she simply adopts because someone expects them of him/her, or they are the line of least resistance;
> in keeping with his or her values;
> achievable within a reasonable time.

The problem-solving approach is geared to the present and the future rather than being preoccupied with past wrongs, mistakes and 'complexes'.

(4) Action

In taking action to deal with a problem, the following strategies help parents or their youngster to make the right move and to verify that they have done so.

Generation of alternatives

Work out as wide a range of possible solutions as you can think of in terms of general strategies (what to do) and, later, specific tactics to implement the general strategy (how to do it). Brainstorming – freely and, at first, uncritically generating as many ideas as possible – can be a help. Let us look at the way David's mother puts the alternatives:

> I could punish David more severely.
> I could ignore him.
> I could try to engage in a calm debate with him.
> I could turn the issue over to his father.
> I could penalize him (take away a proportion of his pocket money each time) without getting into an interminable debate.
> I could negotiate an agreement with him covering the perennial issues we argue over.
> I could look into my own attitudes and feelings toward him. Do I get him going as much as he does me? Am I at fault in some way?

It might be useful to ask others how they would react, or imagine how others might react, if requested to solve a similar problem (e.g. how would his father, aunt or his teacher approach this problem?).

Decision making

Work out the likely consequences of the better courses of action you have put forward. What is the utility of these consequences in resolving the problem as it has been formulated? For example, with regard to the proposed solutions:

- ➤ Punishment doesn't seem to work; in fact it seems to make David more intractable.
- ➤ He'd probably follow me around, arguing more forcibly. Like me, he can be very stubborn.
- ➤ Sounds good, but I find it so hard to keep cool. And we may not be able to resolve things in the heat of the particular confrontation.
- ➤ My husband won't thank me for that; he'll say, 'It's your problem'. I have to cope in my way when David is disobedient.
- ➤ This may work but it could also generate trouble, sulking and tantrums.
- ➤ Sounds a possibility; David can be reasonable when he's in a good mood. The trick is to catch him at the right time.
- ➤ This is painful, but he may have a point when he says he wishes I could hear myself talk to him as if he's an idiot or baby.

Choosing between alternative strategies

Any decision to change is likely to involve benefits and 'costs': benefits for oneself (it is hoped), for significant others, for one's social network. There could be costs to oneself, to others and to one's social setting.

Verification

Try out the most acceptable and feasible-looking solution. Monitor your chosen course of action and its consequences. Try to match the actual outcomes against the hoped-for outcomes; if the match is satisfactory, you 'exit' (to use the jargon) much relieved; if not, you continue to 'operate', which means that you return to the beginning of the sequence of problem-solving operations and start again.

References

Aronfreed, S. (1968). *Conduct and Conscience*. New York: Academic Press.

Barkley, R.A. (1995). *Taking Charge of ADHD*. New York: Guilford Press.

Baumrind, D. (1971). Current patterns of parental authority. *Developmental Psychology Monograph*, *1*, 1–102.

Carr, A. (2001). *Avoiding Risky Sex in Adolescence*. Leicester: BPS Books.

Coleman, J. and Hendry, L. (1999). *The Nature of Adolescence* (3rd edn). London: Routledge.

Coleman, J. C., Herzberg, J. and Morris, M. (1977). Identity in adolescence: present and future self-concepts. *Journal of Youth and Adolescence*, *6*, 63–75.

Erikson, E. (1965). *Identity: Youth and Crisis*. New York: Norton.

Evans, I.M. (1989). A multi-dimensional model for conceptualization for the design of child behavior therapy. *Behavioral Psychotherapy*, *17*, 248–251.

Freud, A. (1958). *Adolescence: Psychoanalytic Study of the Child*. New York: International Universities Press.

Frick, P.J. (1987). Conduct disorder. In T. Ollendick and M. Hersen (Eds.) *Handbook of Child Psychopathology* (3rd edn). New York: Plenum.

Goldstein, S. (Ed.) (1995). *Understanding and Managing Classroom Behavior*. New York: Wiley.

Graham, P. and Rutter, M. (1973). Psychiatric disorders in the young adolescent: a follow-up study. *Proceedings of the Royal Society of Medicine*, *66*, 1226–1229.

Guerin, S. and Hennessy, E. (2001). *Aggression and Bullying*. Leicester: BPS-Blackwell.

Herbert, M. (1987). *Conduct Disorders of Childhood and Adolescence*. Chichester: Wiley.

Herbert, M. (1998). *Clinical Child Psychology: Behaviour, Social Learning and Development* (2nd edn). Chichester: Wiley.

Herbert, M. (2001). Behavioural therapies. In M. Rutter and E. Taylor (Eds.) *Child and Adolescent Psychiatry* (4th edn). Oxford: Blackwell Scientific.

Herbert, M. and Wookey, J. (1998). *Childwise Parenting Skills Manual*. Exeter: Impact Publications, PO Box 342, EX6 7ZD.

Hutter, A. (1938). Endogene en functionelle psychosen bei kindern in den pubertatscjahren. *Kinderpsychiatry*, *5*, 97–102.

Lahey, B.B. and Loeber, R. (1994). Framework for a developmental model of oppositional defiant disorder and conduct disorder. In D.K. Routh (Ed.) *Disruptive Disorders in Childhood*. New York: Plenum Press.

Nielsen, L. (1987). *Adolescent Psychology: A Contemporary View*. London: Holt, Rinehart and Winston.

Patterson, G. (1982). *Coercive Family Process*. Eugene, OR: Castalia.

Robins, L.N. and Price, R.K. (1991). Adult disorders predicted by childhood epidemiologic catchment area project. *Psychiatry*, *54*, 16–132.

Rutter, M. (1979). *Changing Youth in a Changing Society*. London: Nuffield Provincial Hospitals Trust.

Sutton, C. and Herbert, M. (1992). *Mental Health Resource Pack*. Windsor: NFER Nelson.

van Krevelen, D.A. (1971). Psychoses in adolescence. In J.G. Howells (Ed.) *Modern Perspectives in Adolescent Psychiatry*. Edinburgh: Oliver and Boyd.

Webster-Stratton, C. and Herbert, M. (1994). *Troubled Families: Problem Children*. Chichester: Wiley.

Further reading

Dadds, M.R., Schwartz, S. and Sanders, M.R. (1987). Marital discord and treatment outcome in behavioral treatment of child conduct disorder. *Journal of Consulting and Clinical Psychology*, *55*, 396–403.

Dishion, T.J. and McMahon, R.J. (1998). Parental monitoring and the prevention of child and adolescent problem behavior: a conceptual and empirical formulation. *Clinical Child and Family Psychology Review*, *1*, 61–75.

Farrington, D.P. (1995). The development of offending and anti-social behaviours from childhood: key findings from the Cambridge study of delinquent development. *Journal of Child Psychology and Psychiatry*, *360*, 929–1064.

Forehand, R. and McMahon, R. (1981). *Helping the Noncompliant Child: A Clinician's Guide to Parent Training*. New York: Guilford Press.

Hollin, C.R. (1990). *Cognitive-Behavioural Interventions with Young Offenders*. Elmsford, NY: Pergamon.

Kazdin, A.E. (1995). *Conduct Disorders in Childhood and Adolescence* (2nd edn). Thousand Oaks, CA: Sage.

Kendall, P.C. and Hollon, S.D. (Eds.) (1994). *Cognitive-Behavioural Interventions: Theory, Research and Procedures*. New York: Academic Press.

Moffitt, T.E. (1993). Adolescent-limited and life-course persistent antisocial behavior: a developmental taxonomy. *Psychological Review, 100*, 674–701.

Patterson, G.R. (1982). *Coercive Family Process*. Eugene, OR: Castalia.

Patterson, G.R., Reid, J.B. and Dishion, T.J. (1992). *Antisocial Boys: A Social Interactional Approach (Vol. 4)*. Eugene, OR: Castalia.

Robins, L.N. (1966). *Deviant Children Grown Up*. Baltimore, MA: Williams and Wilkins.

Robins, L.N., Tipp, J. and Pryzbeck, T. (1991). Antisocial personality. In N.L. Robins and D.A. Regies (Eds.) *Psychiatric Disorders in America*. New York: Free Press.

Rutter, M. and Giller, H. (1983). *Juvenile Delinquency: Trends and Perspectives*. Harmondsworth: Penguin.

Sanders, M.R. (1996). New directions in behavioral family intervention with children. *Advances in Clinical Child Psychology, 18*, 284–330.

Taylor, T.K. and Biglan, A. (1998). Behavioral family interventions for improving child-rearing: a review of the literature for clinicians and policy makers. *Clinical Child and Family Psychology Review, 1*, 41–60.

Webster-Stratton, C. (1988). *Parents and Children Videotape Series: Basic and Advanced Programs 1 to 7*. 1411 8th Avenue West, Seattle WA, 98119, USA.

Webster-Stratton, C. (1996). Early intervention with videotape modelling: programs for families with oppositional defiant disorder or conduct disorder. In: E.D. Hibbs and P. Jensen (Eds.) *Psychological Treatment Research of Child and Adolescent Disorders*. American Psychological Association: Washington DC.

Webster-Stratton, C. and Herbert, M. (1993). What really happens in parent training. *Behavior Modification, 17*, 407–456.

Hints for parents

Why are adults so prepared to believe the worst of teenagers? Doubtless the reasons are many and varied. Certainly, the context of raising teenagers is an important factor. Parents are facing shifts at this time in their own personal development, from youthful maturity to early middle age. They cannot consider adolescents as young adults, and their problems, without considering the manner in which they interact with their parents. As older (and ageing) adults, they are not without their own preoccupations and anxieties. Most parents are over 30 years old when their first child reaches puberty. Indeed, there are many parents whose children reach their teens when they themselves are in their forties or even fifties.

Parents sometimes feel vulnerable at this stage of life because they themselves are on the slopes (too many see them as downhill) of middle age. Parents are no longer able to claim that they are learners as parents and thus excuse themselves for being baffled at times. And yet an 'L' plate would be very apt given the novelty and, often, the acutely discomforting demands made of their knowledge, resourcefulness and self-esteem by a teenager. It has been observed that a parent's place at this time is 'in the wrong'. And that is no easy place to reside for any self-respecting parent.

But all the evidence points to there being much less deviance, less conflict and less alienation – when it comes to fundamental values – than the stereotypes of adolescents would lead us to expect.

Selective amnesia can also cloud parents' judgements of young people. It would seem reasonable to assume that, since adolescence represents the final phase of childhood and the brink of adulthood, parents' memories would be less dim than they are for other periods. Yet, all too often, parents have to admit in anguish or angry resentment, 'I simply cannot understand my child at all'. But when they say 'cannot' do they really mean 'will not'? For some people, adolescence was a none-too-happy time. They were relieved to put it behind them and (except for a few nostalgic events) forget all about it. And within this forgetfulness not a few unrealized ideals, dashed hopes, unresolved longings and fantasies are buried away. But children grow up and it can suddenly come as a shock when parents see a young adult – emerged from an erstwhile child – reminding them of that painful experience all over again. It is like staring into a mirror when parents look at the teenager; and the image of their self is, at times, threatened.

Some parental preoccupations in mid-life have their parallel in adolescence: a reappraisal of their body image and sense of identity, worries about the future, even new and radical thoughts about the meaning of life. Surely then, there is reason to be sympathetic to the person who is experiencing the transition and change which are central to puberty and adolescence.

Fortunately, there is much that is positive about this stage of life – plusses on which parents can capitalize to build (or restore) a relationship that, on balance, is mainly friendly, supportive and sharing. Children bring forward their positive attributes; they do not suddenly lose these characteristics which most parents have so assiduously nurtured. They also develop new intellectual, social and emotional capacities.

Of course, there are very real problems in adolescence, as there are for every other stage of development. Fortunately, the serious difficulties affect a relatively small minority. Nonetheless, day to day parents are going to face difficulties – some of which are unique: the child's reactions to the new demands of rapid physical change and sexual maturity. There is also the challenge (often an ambiguous one in our society) to be 'grown up'. Others are continuations of earlier difficulties. What puts particular pressure on parents is their perception of some of the awful risks their children may confront at this age.

Adolescence is all about an immature person's journey to self-discovery. In order to help them become adult, parents need to shelter them, in their experiments with life and in the different 'personalities' they try on, from the worst consequences of their mistakes. They can also help them to cope with the disappointments and setbacks (as well as applaud the triumphs) which are part of growing up.

Parent, though, cannot protect young people from mistakes altogether; after all, learning from one's mistakes is what we call experience. Parents will attain a better sense of proportion if they ask themselves what risks they took at their youngster's age. What mistakes did they make? By all means, risks should be discussed with a son or daughter, and limits set when the stakes are high. Parents may be abused for firmness but their actions will be interpreted over the longer term (and this is what is important) as caring.

Doubtless, there will be times when parents' assistance is brushed aside, their advice resisted, and their guidance interpreted as interference. But times of rapid transition are recognized as times when people are open to help, sensibly and sensitively proffered. Contrary to widely held myths about adolescence, teenagers are susceptible to the right sort of intervention, despite their famous reticence and prickliness. Their minds, at this age, are probably as open as they will ever be. But are parents' minds open or closed?

Wise parents have no wish to emerge as victors of battles of will or confrontations with their children. Rather, they wish to win through in the task of supporting children in their journey through adolescence to maturity. A realistic and optimistic (that does not mean Utopian!) view of adolescence plus a sound knowledge of what is happening physically and emotionally to teenagers will allow parents to remain rock solid while their youngster finds his or her adult status. Parents can survive, indeed, enjoy adolescence, by letting the occasional waves of discontent, criticism and rebellion break around them – without breaking them!